Always Dalkey
Always the Sea

New and selected poems

Bernie Kenny

Bernie Kenny

Boland Press

First published in 2011
Copyright @ Bernie Kenny

Boland Press
Grove Mill
Hollyfort
Co. Wexford

www.bolandpress.blogspot.com

A CIP catalogue record for this book
is available from the British Library

ISBN 978-1-907855-03-0

Cover painting *Sea Deep* by Bernie Kenny
Cover design by Boland Press
Printed in Ireland by Conway Media Ltd

These poems sing with art and love. From each 'rare, ordinary day,' they 'come up in flames' of memorable speech, images and understanding. For its fit and beautifully wrought praise for life, for its singing company, this is a book to read gratefully. A book to give, and a book to keep.

Yvonne Cullen

Acknowledgement is given to the following publications where poems, or versions of them, have appeared:

Strands of Silk, Boland Press, (2010)
The Shop
Takahé (New Zealand)

Ode to Light was read on RTE Radio

Bernie Kenny lives in Dalkey, Co. Dublin and holds an M.A. in Creative Writing (Poetry).

Kenny's poems have appeared in publications at home and abroad, including *The Shop, The Stinging Fly, Rising Tide, Wildeside, Away from the Tribe, New Hibernia Review, Mini Sagas, High Tide, Tidings, Strands of Silk* and *Takahé* (N.Z).

Always Dalkey, Always the Sea is the poet's sixth collection following *Poulnabrone* ('02), *Progeny* ('04), *Gone to Earth* ('05) - a book of translations from the Irish poet Greagóir Ó Dúill, *Isle of Thorns* ('06) and *A Walk in Dalkey* ('08).

CONTENTS

Always the Sea

Had we not taken a Detour

Poems as Remedies

Ní bheidh ár Leithéidí arís ann
Our likes will not be again

Notes

Always the Sea

Always Dalkey, Always the Sea

Ní Conmara, daughter of sea-hound,
that is my name. My forebears ashore
built castles of limestone, harried O'Briens,
downed goblets of purebred mead
always listening, watching, wanting the sea,

the sea, my heartbeat, ebb and flow,
revealing, concealing, revealing.

Here at Hawkcliff, sea smells, salt winds
make poems of place names,
Greystones, Bray Head, Killiney, Sugar Loaf.
Sky and sea are mostly grey
but at first light

in winter time I watch them
come up in flames.

I've been to distant places, the Bay of Plenty,
City of Sails, Laguna beach
and always the sea is calling,
barking, begging. Brine lures me in,
gifts me fins, cools my blood, sequins my skin.

Clothe me in fronds of laceweed,
guide me to the Isle of Thorns, glide me home.

Sea lonely blue

I will remember this day.
On a blue and yellow chair
I sit outside and laze away
a Sunday afternoon,
sun on my face.
In silhouette against the sea
valerian sways a drowsy
frieze of pink and green.

My book slips from my hand.
Mademoiselle Emma Roualt
has become Madame Bovary.
Charles is kissing her arm
from shoulder to finger-tips
as, half-laughing, half-annoyed,
she holds him away.

A speedboat cuts a path of foam,
disappears towards Bray.
Go-getting bees, so few this year,
zoom in to plunder new sweet pea.
Barbeque smells and laughter
drift on the cooling air.
I gather sprigs of rosemary.

Encircled

My small home is infatuated with me
and there is nowhere
I would rather be.

These four rooms have walls enough
to hold my portraits of an absent family.
In their beauty they keep eyes on me.

A window paints the Isle of Thorns,
Saint Begnet's church, sea expanse,
a permanence of Wicklow Hills.

Each time I leave I long to return
down twenty steps
let myself in
look out
all there
the sea
cat sleeping
petunia drooping
my universe
rooted in this circle of earth.

Poets' Shed

This room, a summer-house, celebrates
the sea in shells, lobster pots,
paintings of boats, a dolphin
etched on Shanagarry dish,
the only sound pens writing
and from outside the squawk
of gull and children at Whiterock.

A mirror looks through the glass door
frames a rockery, nasturtium gold,
ribbon of white sea, the Sugarloaf
and pink promise in a strip of
evening sky.

Around me, gifts and beachcombed
oddities remember who, where, when.
Conch hears waves at Port of Spain.
Clock ticks Camden Market, Camden Lock,
and, full of themselves, seastones sit
high and dry.

Pinned to the wall, a postcard shows
the Dylan Thomas writing shed
in creative disarray. As my good night
draws near I hear his voice.

To go gentle would be my choice.

Annamaghkerrig 1

I'm airy and winged like sycamore seeds.
These days are mine to touch
to snatch from time.

I idle in woods, walk by lake water.
Leaves jitterbug, pines toss fistfuls of needles.
Mushrooms, enormous and tiny, menace, intrigue.

I creep up narrow stairs to attic rooms
where night-swishings and shivers
whisper sightings of Miss Bunty Worby's ghost.

Dusk greys autumn carnival colours,
crows caw and curse, a lone blackbird sings.
Deóra Dé hang their heads, fade to sticks.

Annamaghkerrig 2

Wistful evening light and quiet
lends me a still life of leaves
fragile in their leaving; a brocade

of sycamore and oak; one sequoia tree
out of its world; blue limestone paths
and shadows green on green.

I memorise the moment.
When darkness closes in, there will be
times when I will need it.

Ennis 1
For Mike

Streets once mine
are transformed by affluence,
their narrow charm one-way traffic'd.
O'Connell on his plinth surveys
boutiques, cafés, superstores,
bright-lit, young,
they do not know me.

Yet these limestone walls,
arched bow-ways, linking lanes,
retain a part of me.
I see again school friends
amble through a sleepy town.
Our convent school is a hotel now.
Where black-wimpled sisters
eyes downcast
told cold-fingered beads,
plainchant and penance fed the soul.

Now four-starred Temple Gate
offers haute cuisine.
My hometown does not know me.

Ennis 2

I am welcome for a while
to holiday in my home town.
My roots are steadfast,
at times like this in the sun
they thirst for a rose-tinted past.

These paths, this sky, church bells
were once all mine,
sugar and gossip across the wall,
feuds old as Clare limestone,
a banner of yellow and blue.

A local by birthright
in a world that was locked
and easy, I knew who was who.
Never having left, never having come,
locals tend the garden. I look on.

Stately Ships of the Meadow

At the close of a sultry day
in a field of startling green
stillness stifles the air.

In single file
udders swinging
tails swatting flies,

eight Friesians move
to shelter under sycamores.
The sky cracks.

Inis Mór

A daughter of the sea
who finds felicity in islands

– any piece of land
surrounded by water –

takes the ferry from Rosaveel
and like a blessing

Aran offers itself to me.

I will remember these days
of light and leisure

viewing again the Man of Aran
seas bounteous and brutal

hearing again the lilt of living blas
proud to understand, be understood

learning druids, herons, beehive huts,
otherworld legends in litanies of stone

being here, wanting nothing more.

Summer Solstice at Liscannor

Soon after dawn, today decides
to be delightful. I'm out early

ears awake
eyes finding miracles.

Larksong climbs a true blue sky
light glitters on the sea

down a green boreen
a farmer sweet-talks

his herd of Friesian,
Charolais and Belgian Blue

to new pastures. Bereft
and hugely stumbling,

loud-lowing mothers mourn
their orphaned calves.

In a pebble I discover
the red, grey, white

of sandstone, limestone,
gleaming quartz – the griancloch,

sacred sunstone of
pagan ritual – and in this place,

on this rare day, I am at one with
weather, rock, and wave.

New Found Out

When Atlantic waves on Kilkee strand
wash away sandcastle years,
I learn to swim.
My father shows me how.
At New Found Out, off the cliffs and deep,
he talks me in, supports me, lets me go
to panic, dog-paddle, breast-stroke,
earn my fins.

And when the tide is out, Duggerna Reef
gives us the Pollock Holes, rock pools
new-filled and shrill with squeals
of children swimming. We step in
from ledges in fear of brown-black
spines of porcupines - our pool,
rain or shine.

To fill the hours we walk the cliffs
past Bishop's Island, by the Diamond Rocks,
the Puffin Hole where we lie prone
and cling in dizzy saltspray gusts.

We shout our loudest in the Amphitheatre,
try snatches of Shakespeare new found out
when Anew Mac Master's strolling players
admit us to their world on mid-summer nights.

Summer after summer
through teenage years,
Lavender's blue, dilly dilly, lavender's green,
when I am king, dilly dilly, you shall be queen.
Sisters, friends, first boyfriends,
dances, heartache, dreams.

Sceilig Mhichíl

From turbulent Atlantic
a Cathedral rises
near perpendicular
jagged green-streaked black
possessed by wings and wails
of puffin, razorbill, kittiwake.

On the rockface
anchorite monks
hacked and hewed
sandstone and shale
six hundred steps
each chiselled chip a prayer.

Sea mist, salt incense
swirls from the summit
reveals two drystone
boat-shaped oratories
six beehive cells
a surprise of fertile green.

'Out, far out of this time
and this world,' *
this shrine of praise and penitence,
place of pilgrimage,
survivor of Viking plunder,
gale whiplash, rainslant,
holds fast.

* George Bernard Shaw

In Jerpoint Abbey

White Monks shiver
within stone walls
of cloister, transept, nave

and tombs of holy men
all interlaced with prayerful
scallop, chevron, beaded scroll,

one hour only permitted
in the warmth of the calefactory
and that hour portioned.

For the celibate
nothing but cold comfort
in his world,

beyond penance, prayer
a vision of the afterlife,
no taste of heaven now.

Foretold

Hammers ring out on boring irons,
torches flare
gunpowder blasts clouds of stone
into Dalkey sound

while Ettie Scott
seated on her granite throne
chides her band of followers:
work well, watch, heed my dreams.

They place their hopes in her
the quarry-man's daughter
who sees The Port of Seven Castles
become an El Dorado.

Under the Long Rock
treasure left in haste
by retreating Danes
will be theirs.

On the Stone Commons
they claim plots
build cabins to store tools.
Day and night they toil.

With dishevelled hair and flashing eye
a game-cock in one hand
in the other a black-hafted knife
the gold-dreamer never smiles.

She awaits a sign.
Out of the darkness
mewling spectres spring
trailing flames and foetid smells.

Demonic pranksters paint cats
with phosphorous, set tails alight,
shatter dreams
leave Ettie broken-hearted.

The wealth-seekers scatter
sell their plots.
Land fever replaces gold fever
and on the Long Rock

maritime mansions rise
Montpelier, Inniscorrig,
Lota, Elsinore,
foretold realms of gold.

Marguerite

After a summer that passed us by
left us white-limbed dreaming of sun

today, under a sky not long wet not long dry,
September comes, brings me

to Inishbofin's shore, a chilly beach
possessed by six fat herring gulls,

anglers tireless as the tide. Their grace,
insouciance, their busyness call to me –

this is the day you were born to seize.
Breathe. Listen. See red-brown kelp

scribble legends on pale sand,
sea-stones cobble a mosaic

and here, all smiles, comes a woman from France,
in her arms the wild, mild smells of autumn,

woodbine, meadowsweet, and marguerites,
a name our tongues can share

on this rare, ordinary day.

Had we not taken a Detour

Bridget and three Patricks

Hearsay tells a tale of West Clare
Capulet and Montague
at ancient variance,

paints Bridget passionate, a dark-haired,
brown-eyed Juliet in forbidden love
with Patrick from another parish.

Under a parental cloud, the couple
make their way to Queenstown,
board the SS Aurania for New York.

Too soon, Patrick's health is ravaged.
There is no cure for T.B.
Bridget takes him home to die

and in eighteen eighty-nine
gives birth to a boy, Patrick,
who became my father.

In another lifetime
two lovers
under a parental cloud

take the boat,
a week-long crossing
from Cobh to the New World.

There, in nineteen fifty-five
our son is born.
We name him Patrick.

1954

Too old now
to re-live it,

the over-brimming, loveful,
lustful, doubtful urgency of it,

the wistful leaving
of career, familiar sweets,

the need to be near you
to talk and talk and not to do

to follow you.

From Cobh we take the boat
the Greek ship Olympia

a long week journey
New York all new

slow train to Montreal.
Snow and sun

and Fall a maple blaze.

Diaspora
For my children

Multicoloured, multisized,
on cobbled shore,
they form a harmonious mosaic
yet clamour, clash, collide
in drenched combat,
claim new ground.

Greys of limestone, granite
black basalt, purple porphyry
quartz translucent, umber, white,
born of boulders, stubborn cliffs,
gouged, ground to round
by countless floods, share histories
of far places, other climates.

Did basalt walk the Causeway of the Giant,
inch across from Fingal's Cave.
Did Ailsa Craig mother the speckled stones
who found landfall here.

Offspring blend or clash
with colours, cultures, creeds,
settle,
claim new ground.

So this is California

where February
is a blaze of bougainvillea,
summer dresses, barbecues,
and white roses a signature
in unexpected places.

Outside my window an orange tree
is laden with sun-gilded fruit
and that trembling glimpse of feather
is a ruby-throated humming bird.
A eucalyptus tree holds on to tattered
leaves, slow to yield to budding green.

Surely Lake Forest has everything,
year-long sunshine is the smile
on friendly faces and yesterday's
surprise of rain a gift,

and here is a multi-acre park,
tree-shade, picnic tables, irrigated
grass, green as a field in Kildare,
dogs are scenting rabbits and from
the foothills of the Saddlebacks
comes a coyote's lonely call.

Cone Art

Until now, a cabin
was a farmyard outhouse
where animals and fowl
were housed, and Corkscrew Hill

a swaying, scary road
in Burren country childhood.
So let me take you
on a corkscrewed drive

higher ever higher to the top
of Big Bear Mountain
to spend the night
in a California cabin

a wooden chalet,
all amenities, wrap-around
decking, beamed ceilings,
wood-burning stove

and all around, towering cedars,
oaks and pines, blue jays,
daffodils in snow,
air-chill like chardonnay.

Amazed to find such sculpted
beauty in cones so large
I choose one, bring memories
and resin fragrance home.

Conspiracy of Daffodils

In the Pink Orchid café,
Shelbourne Falls, Massachusetts,
I scrutinise each face.

Was it the lady of uncertain age
in rainbow skirt, her white hair
jaunty in a pony-tail,

or that young man, all gloomy
purple-greys, spooning three
sugars in his coffee.

Could it be the elderly couple
sharing angel cake
saying nothing.

Nobody knows who,
in the fall of the year,
plotted a secret mission.

By moonlight or by torchlight
a phantom – maybe more than one –
moved along the Mohawk Trail

by the Deerfield river,
pockets bulging, trowel
slicing dew-damp earth,

a twist of the wrist
a tamping foot
and river water chuckling.

In spring,
dazzling the river bank
countless daffodils are dancing.

The Land of the Long White Cloud

is for lovers
of Kiwi
a lifestyle bountiful and easy
Kiwi bird surviving
Kiwi fruit sunripened,
Kiwiana symbolizing
Maori myth and story.

In my kete
flax-woven Kiwi basket
mementoes travel home.
A Koru, frond of silver fern
unfurls new beginnings,
sea-deep blues and greens
ripple on a paua shell,

by ancient tapu
pounamu polished gems,
bracelet, ring, pendant
of green jade, are gifted
to another

and see how Tiki
god of fertility
carved from a Matai tree
brings to mind Sheela na Gig
our stone icon, thighs splayed
on castle wall
or over old monastic door.

In my hand I hold
one perfect scallop shell
chosen from millions
where sunlight sprinkles glitter
on Waihi white shell beach.

Long after a last Haere Ra
to Aotearoa
and my winter-summer holiday
I recall
another earth under my feet
another sky above me.

At the languid close
of a sultry day
thunder growls, lightning
throws a fireworks display
clouds deluge
a miracle of fecund rain

and on a tall magnolia tree
huge blooms, dove-like
vellum-smooth
are poised to fall.

Out of this World

Belching live volcanic mist
into the blue of an untroubled sky,
Whakaari Island in the Bay of Plenty
invites the daring – come,
take the risk, wear gas mask,
stout boots, hard hat, follow the guide.

On unstable rubble step with care,
watch rivers of steam
erupt from earth's crust.
In tortuous swirls
they dance and hiss.

Move closer,
peer into the abyss
where the crater's towering cliffs
shield a lake of simmering menace.

Like flowers – bronzed yellow,
burnished orange, alizarin and blue –
lush beds of sulphur crystals
bloom in fumarole fields.

Visit to South Island

And what was the highlight of your trip?

To be there at Kaikoura
on the shoreline of the wild Pacific,
when, black on black,
an exuberance of fur-seal pups
dozens of black flippers
frolic and bark.

Boisterous toddlers climb, slither
and flop over stone slabs, tumble
together into a rock pool where,
in their element, they are full of grace.

Three blubber-fat mamas
motionless on blue-black boulders,
keep careful watch, while mother cows,
pregnant once again, go out to sea
to feed for two on octopus and krill.

The Loudest Sound

When the fire was raked, the rosary said,
far-distant cousins of the cicada, hearth crickets,
in a far-distant west-Clare cottage
tick-tocked my childhood time for bed.

Daylong from a Kauri canopy
a male voice chorus, clicks, claps, trills
an ecstatic high monotone
of zee-zit-zit-zits like a dentist's drill.

A deafening din to the human ear,
mating calls lure silent females
who respond with a flick of wings.
Destiny fulfilled, males die.

Bright orange, black, April green,
similar species co-exist
heard hidden high,
eyes glow like rubies.

We say they sing of love,
of death, of summer sun.
Theirs is a mating call. They suck
tree sap and sing.

Had we not taken a Detour
we would have missed it

A roadside sign invites us
to the Waterlily gardens at Waihi

by fields of ferns tall as trees
turnings right and left

and we are there.
We stroll through

a maze of painted ponds
where lilies and lush lotuses

cream, buttercup, blush-pink
float on green.

Two peacocks on patrol
strut winding paths

and from time to time
split the silence with a screech.

We linger till light fades
and leaving

carry in our heads
a loveliness of waterlilies.

On Holiday in the City of Sails

I'm spoiled for choice, say no
to surfing, snorkelling, scuba diving,
will not venture out
on speedboat, kayak, dinghy,
wear wet-suit or life-jacket.

Here without a plan
I have no bus to catch
all day to find roads new to me
they welcome me with sun.

I listen to their Maori names,
Wapiti, Aratonga, Remuera,
smell butter-yellow roses
in a Papakura garden.

On Waihi beach shells gleam,
sea like glass, weather perfect
and I am breathing, expect
a poem on the breeze.

If you've been to Lisdoonvarna

to take the waters and gagged
on a glass of sulphur water,
then spare a thought for Rotorua,

where that smell pervades
a geothermal moonscape
of geysers, fumaroles, hissing vents,

of Maori myth and mystery,
the past a constant presence
in a yellow stench.

Watch your step as you skirt
the Devil's Cauldron, a brown pool
belching boiling mud

and Champagne Lake where acid-green,
alizarin, coolblue, crystalise
in clouds of steam.

In haunted dark, spy on sightless
Kiwi, arrow-beaked, hen-sized,
larger than you thought.

Dine if you dare on Hangi kai,
meat earth-oven-cooked by heated rocks,
as the Fianna did in their Fulacht Fia.

I've made it this far

And I am here, close
to the departure gate,
gone through security,
had a Butlers cappuccino
with a chocolate on the side.

I hug my handbag,
check and check again
passport, boarding card, the time,
Gate 5, Gate 5 at 4.45, 4.45.

I've made it this far.
Perched on the edge
of my seat, I pretend
to have found perfect peace.

Poems as Remedies

Recipe

To chase away recession gloom
taste summer in a chip of berries,

indigo and navy blue, begging
to be bitten through to purple juice,

so cold and so sweet, with no apologies,
eat a bowlful on the spot.

Inspired, roll up your sleeves, get baking,
set the scene, dress the table,

chill the chardonnay.
Invite two friends who know.

On bubbling slices of your blueberry pie
delicious scandal will run rife.

Turning Darkness into Light *

The Village bookshop, a house
of mystery, history, crime, romance,
puts poetry on the topmost shelf.
I climb steps. Seduced by colour,
I judge a book by the cover,
a melody of lemon, green,
cerulean blue, and choose
'Dance Dance' for winter evenings.

Watching me from his tartan rug,
white fur purrs possessively.
I name him Pangur Bawn, turn back
pages through the centuries
to a candlelit cell where, side by side,
hunting words, hunting mice,
monk and cat ply their skill.

Lines penned with quill
and herbal ink survive
turning darkness into light.

* From the Irish 7th century poem, *Pangur Bawn*

Ode to Light

Until I had my cataract removed

bluebells were blue. Now in each flower
my new-seeing eye finds sapphire

edged with sky, and stamens
are bell-pulls dipped in gold,

a granite wall shows glints of mica,
grains of feldspar and quartz

and, puddling a reflection, cherry blossom
paints a watercolour on the path.

I think of Monet losing his sight,
waiting too late,

an artist entranced by the garden he made,
mutations of light

on plant, pond, sky. I feel his rage
kicking his boot

through canvases of waterlilies,
in despair.

His vision remains, mine to view.

Sean-nós Dancer

Alone, freelance,
in tune with fiddler's bow
he takes the floor
listening feet hop step
stamp an age-old story
answer the dance
his fathers danced
on stone on stone,
arms loose, eyes closed,
in tranced proud ritual
of motion, out of himself,
homespun and powerful
the dancer dances on.

The beat charges through me
and I who haven't danced
for years am transported,
alive, awake, while
in the thump of dancing feet
a poem speaks.

Gareth

Now that you are walking, full-time,
you have the run of the house.

I find you in my bedroom, staring
at the sliding mirror door
in wordless surmise.
I put words in your mouth -

Who is that wearing my brown trousers
my blue socks and the new shoes
Mammy got from the man in the shop.

Fás aon Oíche
Growth of one Night

Showered in morning dew
I love the ivory smell of you

and how you hide from me
play peek-a-boo

now I don't see you
now you are here

inviting me to wrap five fingers
round your smooth cold skin

pluck you from the ground
hold you tenderly

all mine all new and pure
viewing the world for the first time.

Kernels of Wisdom

In October chill I find,
in a grove of sycamores,
a surprise of hazel bushes

and I, who forget so much,
am a child once more
stretching to pick nut clusters

in their frilly green caps,
doubles, trebles, occasional fours,
and who will be first to fill a school satchel.

We crack open gold shells
stone on stone, gobble up nuts,
pointy and white, not yet fully ripe,

unaware and uncaring
how the Ancients knew hazels
brought wisdom,

how they made baskets and
thatching, staffs for pilgrims
rods for divining

or why, found in a lake
fringed with nine hazels,
Fionn's Salmon of Knowledge was wise.

Steele's Rock

November, and the day dies young,
leaves the world to darkness and to S.A.D.

White horses prance on fuming seas,
gloom lingers on the beauty of bare trees

and in the daylight robbery
of one bright hour.

These witching nights the Púca is about,
polluting late berries, colluding

with seasonal disorder to perfect
the black art of wither-shrivel-rot.

I place my hopes on a nut-brown gelding
running today at Punchestown.

If Winter comes

I wake to blinding polar light
my world made new

nothing more white
nothing more pure

I search for colour, comfort colour,
reds cherry-ripe

one green sprouting thing
and in a pot, iced sugar muffin,

a daffodil unfazed
sends up cool blades

nodding a yellow bud
to spring.

My house is full of objects I once loved

The time has come to cull.

Fengshui says I must dejunk,
let life force flow unhindered
by too much stuff. True,

but what to dump and leave
no heartache, no trace
of why or when or where.

Would I miss that blue, still pretty
pottery jar, chockfull of useless
and disgraceful things,

that once-prized carriage clock
in need of nothing more
than batteries and brasso,

gizmos seldom used, a wok, a waffle iron,
cherry stoner, plug-in potato peeler,
a soda stream, an onion-blossom maker

and baubles,
each with a tale to tell,
why should they outlive me

in an unloved box.
Let them shine again
in other histories.

The Confucius of the Kitchen

whose Magnum Opus acquired
the circulation of a bestseller
by representing Home - the place where
we are loved and fed - became the benefactress
of a million housewives, rescuing them
from perplexity and woe.

Her book provided recipes, solutions
to domestic problems, remedies galore
in homes where the Mistress of the House
took responsibility for its management,
kept a watchful eye on her full complement
of staff, none of whom would answer back

in their downstairs world of Monday coppers,
blisters, blue, beeswax, mulligatawny soup,
and countless skills – how to skin a rabbit,
fillet fish, truss a partridge, wring a turkey's neck.
The duties of a laundrymaid made her
sound like the head boilerman of a steamship.

Mrs Beeton, the housewife's guide,
philosopher and friend, never cooked.

Les Parapluies

Let it rain,
raise blue umbrellas to the rain
on this Spring day in Paris
when all the world is gay,

let your brush caress
the pattern of curves and angles
you make of handles, furls,
round limbs and Renoir faces,

touch them with liquid light,
gleam gold on auburn hair,
on lifted folds of a young girl's
dress as she steps lightly

out of the picture, so lightly
you say she could walk
on grass without hurting it.

As expected

Year in year out
what I love about you
is how you keep your promise

how our elders named you
lus an chromchinn
and how you slyly bow

your golden heads
while loudly trumpeting
an ode to spring.

For John aged five-and-a-quarter

Granny,
we're moving to California, you say,
and from a blaze of purple-pink

you choose one hydrangea flower,
then with a smile all yours
present me with a fragile star.

Ruth

A willow weeping on a lily pond,
slender, strong, full of grace
in blue-skyed California
your leaves will give you shade

out of your strength
a place called home will come
and spreading branches hold
your world in close embrace.

When I peel onions

I cry for the child I was,
playing with chanies
finding late strawberries
and getting in the way
while father saved his onion crop
spread out to dry.

All winter long
plucked from Gallic traces,
onions flavoured soup, stews
and every savoury thing.

On Lenten Fridays, they
made dinner sautéed in butter
with parsley sauce, potatoes,
great appetites.

For Easter Day boiled onion skins
dyed our hard-boiled eggs
Rhode Island red and we were eight
around the breakfast table
when the sun danced.

Ní bheidh ár Leithéidí arís ann
Our likes will not be again

Fiche Blian ag fás

I

Twenty years a-growing
twenty years blooming,
twenty years stooping,
twenty years declining,
that, my grandfather told me,
is how the life of man is divided.

Without doubt youth is a fine thing
and mine is not over yet.
Born and bred in the Great Blasket,
when I was only half a year old
my mother died, God rest her soul,
and I was fostered by a woman
in Dingle until I was seven.

Tis well I remember the happy day
when my father and two aunts came
to take me home. They spoke only Irish.
An egg would not have broken under
my feet for the lightness of my heart.
In my first suit of clothes,
new shirt, shoes and cap,
I am made into a man with finery.

II

The aunts smother me with kisses
I don't want, call me a stór –
aren't women the very devil for plamás.
When we reach the quay what do I see
but up to twenty black beetles, each twice
as big as a cow and one heading for me –
our curragh to take us home my aunt says
snatching another kiss from me.

In we get and off we go, the boat
bobbing like a cork on the ocean.
Before long I have a fine view of the Island,
echoes of dogs barking in the coves,
a corncrake croaking craoch craoch
and people running like ants down
every path to welcome me home.
My house delights me and it white
with lime inside and out. There I find

two sisters, two brothers, my grandfather
looking at me all smiles, a glowing fire
warming every corner and on the table
a wholesome meal, potatoes and yellow bream.
When the lamp is lit, the house fills
with music and dancing loud enough
to wake the dead. Everyone claps when
out of my mouth come my first
words of Irish – 'mo ghrá go deó thú.'

cont.

III

Next morning my grandfather straddles
the ass and takes me with him
for a load of turf, I making wonder
of everything I see – herring gulls
in hundreds around fishing trawlers,
larks warbling over the heather,
lambs frisking and playing tricks
like children let out of school.

My grandfather is full of stories
and pride in his native island,
a place of peace and plenty,
our own food and clothes,
the pick of the shore, the hunt of the hill,
the fish of the sea, the wool of the sheep
and the devil-a-bit to buy but
a bandle of tobacco for thruppence.

At school I make friends with Tomás,
he takes me hunting rabbits, puffins,
eggs of gulls and guillemots,
he buckjumping like a mountain goat,
I nervous at first but before long
the happiest hunter on the hills of Kerry
and the dirtiest. We strip and dip
in a bog pool and head for home.

Dock–leaves are closing for the night,
sea-birds homing to their young
rabbits rushing through the ferns,
and a lonesome look on the ravines.
Lamps are lit in the village,
houses reflected in the ocean
and a big moon climbing yellow as gold.

IV

For days before Ventry Races
there is talk of nothing else. On the day
Tomás and I are up with the chirp
of the sparrow racing to the quay
and in we jump to Sean Thaidhg's
curragh. When we land Tomás
is lost in astonishment. By my soul
says he, isn't Ireland wide and spacious.

The strand is mirth and merriment,
clatter and clamour, tumult and turmoil
and four curraghs lined up to race.
Like a swarm of bees on a fine day
crowds all shouting, praising the ancestors,
praising the winners, Up Cuas, Up Cuas,
one man up to his waist in the water,
then away with them all to the pub.

cont.

V

At old Kate Liam's wake, when I see her
stretched out straight as a candle
under a white sheet and old women
keening olagón olagón, I shake with fear
that she might rise up before me
but soon I am enjoying the night,
young and old telling stories, laughing,
crying, merry with the drink
and a pipe in every mouth till sunrise.

VI

A great change has come over the Island,
young people have left for America,
my brothers, sisters, Tomás all gone
and I too make my way to the far away
city of Dublin to join the Civic Guards.
It is two long years before I return
on holiday, happy as a starling
to see my home again.

Grass is growing on the paths for lack of walking,
no trace remains of the red patches
on the sandhills made by dancing feet.
I stand at the door, the lamp is lit,
my father and my grandfather
sit on either side of the fire.

Will no one say their Name

Now she is gone, yellowing snapshots
lie unmourned in a forgotten box.
Will no one claim these images:

a mother at her cottage door
in west Clare by the sea, waves
her son a last God bless

and he, a suitcase in his hand,
will sail tomorrow to the next parish over,
will not see home again;

the school group, eighteen girls
saying cheese in pinafores,
black stockings, laced-up shoes;

newly weds, she sitting stiffly
holding her bouquet, he standing stiffly,
a cufflinked wrist on her bare arm;

babies in great-grandma's christening robe,
First Communion angels for a day,
graduates in gown and mortar board.

Will no one say their name.

In Kilfane Graveyard

headstones lean towards me,
look at me, they say,
speak my name.

Here lieth Lawrence Flynn, 75,
with Lawrence his grandchild
who died at birth.
    No other.
    A broken line.

Aged one hundred and one
John Barry departed this life
on January first, 1855
     beyond the horror
     of potato blight.

John Elliot Power,
veteran of the Boer war,
boasts insignia
sculpted in stone –
a buckled belt,
binoculars, helmet and sword.
     'He fought a good fight.'

On fullmoon nights
when yew trees
throw long shadows,
do ghosts with names
now seldom used
possess the earth –
                    Susannah, Jacob,
                    Eli, Gwendolene,

children in pinafores
men in waistcoats
thumbing their watch chains,
young ladies, hair upswept,
demure in high ruched blouses,
widows in their sombre weeds,
                    a procession led
                    by the most recently interred.

First School, Ballycar N.S., 1929
i.m. my father, Patrick McNamara

Beyond 3 Rs, we endured
parsing and analysis, Euclid,
Latin verbs, trains overtaking
at deranged speeds,
'Classic Myth and Legend'
transported us to Greece.
We tended plants and trees.
To click of steel, in plain and purl
socks cast off toe and turned heel
and there was fun and fear of blame,
of bamboo cane.

All questions in the penny catechism
commanded prompt replies,
big words, big lists, big sins,
seven deadly. I hear them still:
pride, covetousness, lust, anger,
gluttony, envy, and sloth.
And seven gifts of the Holy Ghost:
wisdom, understanding, counsel,
fortitude, knowledge, piety
and fear of the Lord.
Unsure which list was which,
we took a chance on one.

Walls were a world of maps,
continents oceans away,
further than dreams that one day
I would wrap up against Canadian snow,
pick apples in Tasmania,
mingle with throngs in Tokyo.

Past Times

Today's Irish Times comes with a copy
of its first edition, four pages packed
with ads, each a word-picture
presented with eloquent politeness
at a time when the customer
was always right.

I am reminded of a summer day
in the nineteen thirties, my mother
is buying dress material for me
at Matthew Kennedy's Drapery, The Square
– what a grand place it seems –
she is greeted by name, seated
at the counter where bale after bale
of fabric is unwound, its virtues
expounded on with pleasantries
about her health, the weather, me.

Her choice is rose-sprigged organdie,
then comes the business of settling
the account. Folded notes are borne aloft
by rope and pulley in a round wooden box.
Up it flies to the holy of holies
where Matthew himself holds court.
In due course, the box comes rattling back
with change, receipt and thanks.

Today at Penneys, waiting to pay
for a white t-shirt and black tights,
I stand in line with nineteen others
until the girl with the purple streaks
nods me to her till, scans my laser card
and tells me to have a great day.

The Ballroom of Romance

Girls of all ages, in smiles
and flower-print dresses,
sit side by side on benches

shyly watching
boys of all ages
stand shyly watching them.

Everybody loves somebody sometime.
The band strikes up.
Boy chooses girl. On with the dance.

Has she *grown too old to dream*.
Has she, in twenty years, waltzed
away her youth, her beauty, her need.

Must she *save the last dance*
for whiskey kisses and a moot proposal
under a mocking moon.

Leaving

As the days grow shorter, crisper,
swallows all a-twitter on phone lines
are booking their flights.

In shades of apricot, russet and gold,
leaves leave an abundance of berries,
go out dancing.

Present.
Then absent.
No mourning.

What a way to go.

My Photos travel back

This one stops at Brittas Bay,
a navy-blue sky holding off rain,
four girls, nineteen,
out for the day.

Every syllable is aching as I name
Myra, Marykate, Noreen,
four of us smiling,
one of us breathing.

Now, years later
I conjure up the past
and celebrate
that June-soft, water-lit day,

a radiance of friends,
frivolous and flowering,
I, the longlived, dream
them up, vivid, eager

with gossip and laughter,
our slant on what is new,
sharing lipstick, Evening in Paris,
high heels, boyfriends.

Look, I'm wearing Myra's
primrose peplum dress
and like a gypsy she swishes
my red taffeta skirt.

Our bare legs are sunstarved white,
our hair, brushstroked
a hundred times
tangles the breeze.

Breathless, we babble big issues,
nylon stockings,
Hiroshima, Daz,
Mick Delahunty's band.

The Empty Chair

I sit at my side of the fire
hold a box unopened
delay the moment.

The lid yields easily
to petal dust
a skeletal leaf

and we are once upon a time
young and beautiful
the day is ours, the lake,

sun-dappled shade
and honeyed scent
of wild woodbine.

All Souls

From every corner comes the hum
of 'how've you been' and 'did you hear',
spangles of laughter, champagne toasts,
hints of scandal, tall stories.

Against night spells
we close the doors, until
a charm of mini-witches,
devils, spidermen comes
trick-or-treating in a whoosh
of shrivelled leaves.

Fireworks cackle and hiss
and like a dance macabre
a wild wind waltzes
with stripped twigs
and the moon is full.

No ghost sits at our feast
but thoughts of a loved one gone
float on buoyant spirits
and we say – it seems like
only yesterday she was
the life and soul.

No greater Love

Miki Ando
In the minutes between earthquake
and tsunami, a town clerk
repeatedly told people on her PA system
to flee, before her office was engulfed
and she was washed out to sea.

Motoko Onodera
A high-school teacher, married, expecting
her first baby, having made sure her
students were safe, sped by car to warn
swimmers on the shore. All are missing.

Mitsuru Sato
The manager of a seafood factory
led twenty Chinese workers to the safety
of a shrine on high ground. He drowned.

Kimihiro Ochikawa
The only doctor in the stricken village of Noda,
whose clinic was destroyed, lives with
survivors, spends all of every day
tending sick and elderly.

Tokiko Kitano
One hundred kilometres from the nuclear plant
at Fukushima a sixty-year old woman
shares her house with seventeen refugees,
and, in sub-zero temperatures, takes food
from door to door in a wheelbarrow.

Darkness

curtains the picture window.
The pine tree creaks,
sheds rusty needles
on a drooping garden.

With so much living
still to do, you who knew
when to plant and pick
and prune,
have gone off-stage.

Na Páistí marbha, Achill
The dead Children

No breath
on stone-strewn ground
where no-name babies lie

no sound
but high larksong
no milestones.

'There was a Child went forth' *

and everything she saw and touched,
all she heard, every scent and dream
is part of her:

the yellow walls of a tall house,
love in the lick of a collie's tongue,
sea-holly's silver spikes and flowers,
a parcel in the post, Dick Whittington,
limestone, hazel bush, thistledown,

a robin rigid in her pet cat's claws,
lamp black throwing monsters on the wall,
an avalanche of snowflakes in a paperweight,
panic in bumper-car attack, cackle of sparks,
scorched crimson, electric blue,

hours in a rock pool discovering crabs,
sea-urchins, corkscrewed reflections,
pebbles like gems, fishy smells
words in her head,
                    plumduff,
          papoose   poppycock,
                    lilo   lilibolero
          timbuktu
                    tomahawk

time blown away on a dandelion clock.

                              * Walt Whitman

Three Sisters in their Eighties revisit Kilkee

where as children we holidayed each year,
three summer weeks of many weathers
wishing to stay, swim, play for ever.

Low-tide and Duggerna Reef appears,
reveals three pools, the Pollock Holes,
refilled by moon power with pristine water.

Where once we skipped barefoot
we now pick our steps
on slick terraces and ledges.

We reach the Diamond Rocks,
no diamonds here but memories etched
on crazy paving from cliff-top to sea.

On the deserted beach
bare broken sea-shells lie, halves
once hinged together for a time.

Epilogue

In the rooms of her life
walls hold moonlit silence
histories sleep in shadows.

Before the Púca comes

Back through the decades
I chase the scent of blackberries,

legs mapped red by nettle stings,
the bull one field away

as purple fingers hack
through briars and scary cobwebs

to reach the fattest, blackest,
taste sweetness wild and musky

till, berry by glistening berry,
my stained-glass jamjar bleeds.

At Eighty-two

You who travel alone
go on African safaris, swim all weathers,
now down-sized, fragile as a folded bird,

you sit, take unsteady steps,
smile me a welcome, seeming
in aloneness to be content

here where uneasy quiet settles
on patients who live out long days
with little to say of hope or despair.

Your eyes, your inwardness
stop my breath with a blade of pain,
we talk of the past, you fill gaps,

no tomorrow, today is tablets, therapy,
the dreadful comfort
of day and night care.

Gift

By stealth the season is shifting,
on its breath portents of change,

by the back door the Rowan tree
is turning red berries on.

Days fly like leaves, yet there are times
when an hour grows huge and deep.

Reflected in stillness,
how strange, how hopeful

are scraps of old poems,
young faces, the past.

November

In this morning's post
I receive unbidden

the penny catechism of my youth,
same blue-green cover,
pages tissue-thin, numbered
one to sixty-three,
all asking, answering
questions on the cosmic why

and I am a child again,
uncomprehending,
learning every page by heart,
sing-song replies verbatim,
big words, big lists, big sins
– seven deadly –
on the tip of my tongue.

Behind Killiney Hill the sun
sets earlier each day
and I am mindful of you,
at peace when the end drew near,
you simply said –
we must believe.

The Question

When no-one is listening
do you ask
how you would wish to go,

asleep in your bed
unaware that in the night
your spirit has benignly fled,

or would you rage,
'rage against the dying of the light.'

The end might come when you
are running a marathon,
tending your prize marrows,

or ticking
the Great Skellig
off a list.

Like Jade Goody
live on T.V.
would you break taboos

or dare to end it all
at a Swiss clinic,
'go gentle into that good night.'

Birthday

With gratitude I accept your seat
on the crowded bus. You're telling me
what I should know, yet I believe
I am still too young to be old.

Older yes. Glimpsed from behind
might I be mistaken for, say, sixty-nine
or seventy or, at the most, not a day
over seventy-five.

That withered woman
in the mirror I do not recognise,
am I not too hopeful, too busy,
too insufficiently wise.

You advise I take more rest.
With help from some spare parts
I consider myself fit, but promise
to avoid as best I can

being required to wear
life jackets, thermal underwear, skis,
or go on African safaris to stare
at photogenic beasts.

Until I am old – and that will be
decided when I get there –
I'll wear long vintage dresses
in alarming colours,

trust my shopping trolley
with essentials and now and then
recall the auburn girl
who danced with life,

turned her back and waltzed away.
Imagine her surprise
if she could see me now
at eighty-five.

Notes

Page 5
Deóra Dé - God's tears (Irish). Fuchsia

Page 10
blas - flavour (Irish). Clear musical articulation

Page 29
Haere Ra - farewell (Maori)
Aotearoa - New Zealand (Maori)

Page 35
Fulacht Fia - clinkered cooking pit (Irish)

Page 50
lus an chromchinn - plant of the bent head (Irish). Daffodil

Page 56
Fiche blian ag fás - *Twenty years a-growing*, a book by
Muiris Ó Súilleabhán (1933)

Page 57
a stór - my darling (Irish)
plamás - flattery (Irish)
mo ghrá go deó thú- you are my love forever (Irish)

Page 60
olagón - wail (Irish)

Page 81
Púca - a malevolent fairy who spat on berries in November
making them unsafe (Irish)